MW01518456

LOCAL HAUNTS
Boulder City, Nevada

Based on interviews and research
conducted by David Weatherly

Eerie Lights Publishing
Eerielightspublishing.com

LOCAL HAUNTS
Boulder City, Nevada

Based on interviews and research
conducted by David Weatherly

Copyright © 2022, David Weatherly & Eerie Lights Publishing
All rights reserved.

No part of this publication may be reproduced or transmitted in any form
or by any means, mechanical or electronic, including photocopying and
recording, or by any information storage and retrieval system, without
permission in writing from the author or publisher (except by a
reviewer, who may quote brief passages in articles or reviews).

ISBN: 978-1-945950-33-9 (Paperback)

Published by:

EERIE LIGHTS
Eerie Lights Publishing
Eerielightspublishing.com

Cover design:
Gerald Vance
adVANCEd Creations

Editor: Jerry Hajewski

Book layout/design: SMAK
www.smakgraphics.com

Printed in the United States of America

Also by David Weatherly

Table of Contents

Boulder City
NEVADA

Foreword

Boulder City, Nevada is HAUNTED. But many of the people there don't want to discuss that. It took me a while to figure out why.

The town was created to house the Hoover Dam workers. These men were entrusted with huge, dangerous explosives and expensive equipment. If there were any hint of a worker being unstable, or insane, that worker was promptly removed from the project.

It's always risky to admit you have seen a ghost. Some people will immediately question your sanity. Therefore, talking about it gained the workers nothing, yet they could lose a valuable job.

And so, an unspoken tradition was passed down through generations of Boulder City residents. Almost everyone had heard the spooky stories but discussing them was taboo. Even worse, some residents believed that dwelling on ghost stories might be bad luck—attracting death and misfortune.

Thus, for generations, the phantoms of Boulder City were only mentioned in whispers.

As a Paranormal Investigator, when I began interviewing people in Boulder City, I was often viewed with suspicious eyes. It seemed everyone wanted to tell me something, but that culture of secrecy was hard to break.

After all, the United States government owns 85% of Nevada—more than any other state. And the world's most top-secret projects take place there, often around the infamous Area 51.

There are so many tales of UFOs, spirits, and weird creatures in the state that a zone, known as the eerie "Nevada

Triangle," connects Las Vegas to Reno, Nevada and Fresno, California. It's even more paranormally active than the Bermuda Triangle. Thus, it seems fitting that Nevada became a state on Halloween—October 31, 1864.

The ground is filled with gold, silver and other highly-conductive metals and minerals. Although it's called the "Silver State," Nevada is the 4th largest producer of gold in the world and the largest in the United States. There is a connection between paranormal activity and electromagnetic anomalies, and the landscape of Nevada naturally pulsates with erratic, electric fields.

Boulder City is a quiet, charming place with a history of tragedies. Building the Hoover Dam was a dangerous project, claiming many lives. Additionally, the stress surrounding the work triggered other problems. Tempers were short in the scorching desert heat. And although alcohol was legally banned, it was heartily consumed in town, adding fuel to domestic problems resulting in murder and suicide.

The combination of Nevada's geology and the dry air crackling with electrostatic energy, along with the tense, human drama, culminated in the perfect conditions for a haunted little town. Dreary spirits lingered, and the landscape charged them, powered them, allowed them to manifest at times.

My research led me to ultimately create the "Haunted Boulder City Ghost & UFO Tour." It's the first paranormal walking tour in the city's history. I was uncertain what the response would be, but I sold 2,000 tickets right off the bat. This was proof that the region was finally ready to talk about the secrets of the past.

In this book, my good friend David Weatherly, one of the world's greatest authors, has given you some of the information from the tour, plus some other tales that go even further. It is an easy read, and a great overview of what makes Boulder City such a special place.

Whether you're a lifelong local, or a tourist in town for the weekend, our goal is to surprise and educate you.

During the day, you can stroll the streets of historic Boulder

City enjoying wine bars, antique stores, and quirky gift shops. All is warm and calm. All the people are smiling. It's an old-fashioned, all-American time capsule.

But when the sun goes down, and the dark streets become quiet and desolate, you will hear things and see things you cannot explain. Just be patient and still.

In these pages, David Weatherly will tell you why these strange phenomena exist in Boulder City. And if you haven't already, please join us for a walking tour. It's an easy walk, suitable for all ages.

We'll do our best to show you—in person—why Boulder City is a paranormal dream come true.

Joshua P. Warren

Las Vegas, Nevada

December 2021

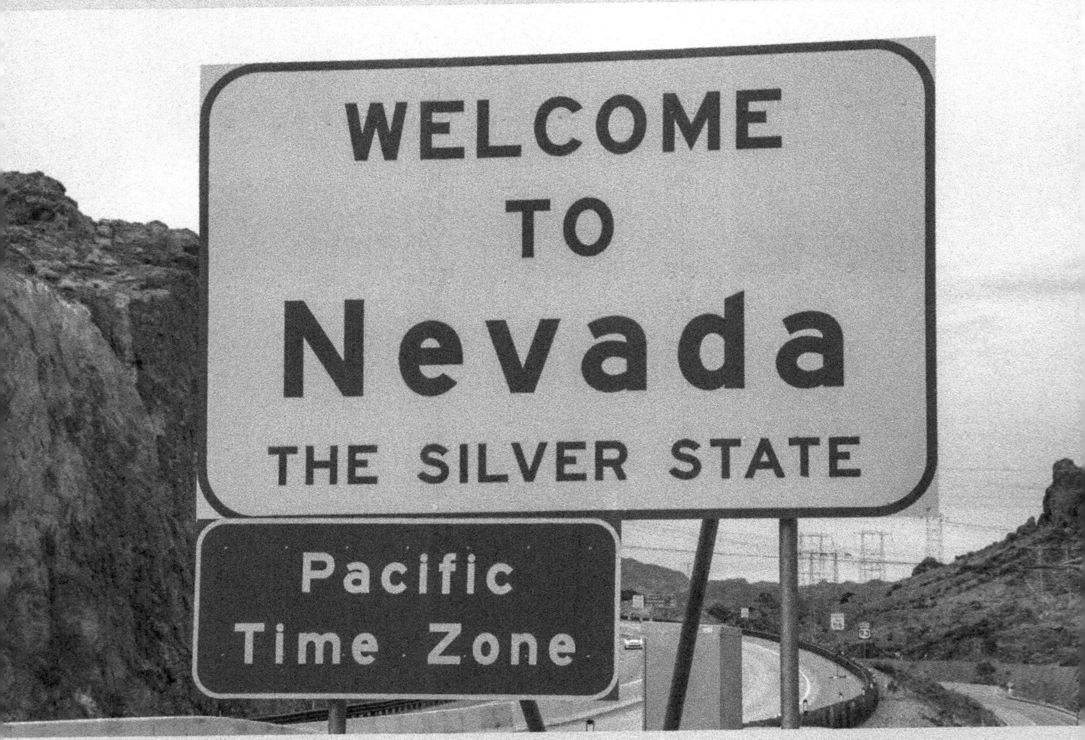
WELCOME
TO
Nevada
THE SILVER STATE
Pacific
Time Zone

Introduction

I first visited Boulder City many years ago. It was during a road trip through the southwest. The peaceful red deserts of Arizona gave way to the paler brown and tan palate that marks southern Nevada. It was dusty and arid, and the windows were down as I headed for the bright lights of Las Vegas. I crossed the Hoover Dam and made a stop in the small town of Boulder City. It was late at night, and I found myself in a ghost town, one that seemed to be frozen in time.

Near the center of town, I found the historic Boulder Dam Hotel. It was a spot I wanted to check out because of the ghostly legends associated with it. (More on that later). I parked downtown and walked the streets for a bit, taking in the quiet and feeling the history of one of Nevada's most unique towns.

Fast forward, years later, and I can assure you that Boulder City still retains the charm and sense of timelessness that it had when I stopped for my first visit that night. Don't get me wrong, there's not a lack of modern conveniences, and there are plenty of shops and restaurants to visit for good food and entertainment in Boulder City. It's a comfortable town and there are good reasons that people are drawn to it. But the city's atmosphere also has an undertone, one that gives you a sense not just of history, but of hidden things.

When I learned that my friend and colleague Joshua P. Warren was starting a ghost tour in the small city, I knew a couple of things. One, it would be successful because Joshua doesn't do anything halfway. Two, I knew that he would find it...interesting. As he so succinctly pointed out in his foreword for this book, people in Boulder City are, at the least, often reluctant to share their supernatural encounters. Nevertheless, strange experiences do happen in the town it's just a matter of rooting out the ghostly tales.

Over the years, I've spent some time in Boulder City talking to the people, going to the historic locations, and wandering the town, often in the late hours of the night. In this book, you'll hear some of the paranormal tales I've collected from the city and, I hope, you'll get a sense of the unique slice of America that Boulder City represents. Although it's a modern place in some ways Boulder City hasn't changed that much, and the residents seem to like it that way.

Introduction

Boulder City circa 1932

Boulder City

About thirty miles southeast of Las Vegas you'll find "Clean, Green Boulder City," a historic town with a fascinating and unique history.

Boulder City may sit in the shadow of Las Vegas, but you'll find there are some stark differences between it and its mega popular neighbor. First off, there's no gambling in Boulder City. That's right—no table games, no cards, no slot machines. It's one of only two places in the state where gambling isn't legal. (The other is Panaca, three hours north of Boulder City.)

The town was built during the tumultuous 1930s, a time of prohibition and the Great Depression. When the government finalized plans for the construction of the massive dam on the Colorado River, hordes of people flocked to the area, hoping to land a job working on the project. All those men and their families would have to live somewhere, and the government decided to build a planned community to house them.

Saco Rienk de Boer, an architect who had been a planner for Denver, Colorado, was hired to mastermind a planned community for those working on the dam; thus, Boulder City was born, a structured place with strict codes that would exemplify clean living. Unlike its close neighbor, Las Vegas, Boulder City would not be a den of vices. Boulder City would have no liquor and no gambling. The emphasis was to be on clean living in hopes that the workers would behave better and work more efficiently.

The construction of the dam was seen as a sign of optimism, a hopeful sign of jobs, prosperity, and a brighter future for the country; and the project employed thousands of workers over the years it was constructed.

The city was planned to accommodate five thousand workers, and, while it has grown over the years, it remains small with a population of just over fourteen thousand people.

In 1983, the Boulder City Historic District, an area roughly bordered by Nevada Highway, Avenue L, Date, and 5th streets, was added to the National Register of Historic Places. Today, the town remains a popular tourist destination and people travel from all over the world to see the Hoover Dam.

The city's controlled-growth policy has helped it keep its small-town atmosphere. There are parks and trees that offer some shade from the desert heat. In town, you'll find plenty of shops, art galleries, old fashioned eateries, and stores, and all the modern conveniences you might want. And like any historic town, you'll find ghostly legends.

The dam and its history are ever present in Boulder City, and some say the spirits of some of those who worked on the massive project remain as well. Many houses around town are purported to be haunted, and accounts range from apparitions to moving objects, cold spots, and other ghostly activity. But ghosts are not always a comfortable topic, and many residents simply don't want to discuss their hauntings publicly, preferring to keep their tales between close friends and family. Still, stories do get out.

Take the old apartments on Ash Street. They date back to the city's early days and were originally constructed to house men working on the dam project. Over the years, they've developed quite a reputation.

One Boulder City resident named Allicia says that the local haunted hotel is nothing compared to the activity on Ash Street. Commenting on an article on the Living Las Vegas website, Allicia reports that the apartments can be downright frightening:

"Very crazy stuff happens there. You can just feel something is strange when you are in the apartments. There have been doors slamming, the feeling of being watched, the feeling of a rush of cold air...and most chilling...a steak knife floating just a few inches off the kitchen counter. If you want to rent one of the apartments, I wouldn't sign a very long lease."

It's not just inside the apartments either. Another woman I spoke with told me about the experience she had while living in Boulder City. Alice lived in town for a few years before she got a job offer out of state and left. She says she has a lot of fond memories of her time in the city, but the night she and a friend were walking on Ash Street has remained her most intense one.

"It was a beautiful night in late September 2012. The sun had mostly gone down and there wasn't much of anyone around, nobody on the block with us at the time. We were walking slow and talking. My friend stopped in the middle of her sentence and stopped walking. I was looking at her, thinking something was wrong and I started asking her what was the matter. She didn't answer, she was just staring ahead. I turned and saw what she was looking at. There were two men coming toward us. They were in work clothes, and they looked like they were kind of dragging along, like they were extremely tired. But the thing was, they were half transparent. You could see through them!"

Alice said the men looked as though they were talking to each other, and she had the impression they had "just gotten off work after a long, hard day." The men got to within about ten feet of Alice and her friend. The two women had not moved, too stunned at what they were seeing to react. As they watched, the two men faded from sight as if they were smoke on the wind.

Perhaps Alice and her friend saw a residual impression of men who had worked on the Hoover Dam. The encounter left her puzzled, but she never felt threatened during the incident. As she reports:

"We didn't feel scared, just sort of dumbfounded by what we saw. I know they were ghosts, but I sure can't explain it. Whenever I think about Boulder City, I think about those ghosts."

Alice and her friend had a very benign encounter and the spirits they saw seemed to simply be going about their business, but such isn't always the case with the departed; some are much more troubled....

Housing built for dam workers

A Murderous Affair

Boulder City is rated one of the safest cities in the United States, and violent crime, especially murder, is rare in the city limits. But there have been some notable exceptions. The city's first murder occurred in 1937 and the killer was a woman.

George Nusser and his wife, Grace, moved from Los Angeles to Boulder City and rented a company house on Ash Street. Their marriage was a troubled one, and reportedly, George frequently beat Grace, inflicting serious damage to her. As if such suffering weren't enough, George was also unfaithful, and it wasn't long after they had moved to Nevada that he took up with another woman.

As if things couldn't get any worse for Grace, she received a phone call one day from George's attorneys informing her that he had filed for divorce.

On April 27, 1937, a drunken Grace went to the house on Ash Street, the one she had tried to make a comfortable home, and walked quietly inside. George was asleep when Grace pulled out the .38 pistol she had bought and shot him dead.

Grace covered George's body with a white sheet and calmly left the house. She drove to a local gas station where, covered in blood, she paid for her purchase with blood-soaked dollar bills. Then, she drove out to the dam where she passed out in her car.

A local ranger found her that night and Grace fired off two shots at the man before he was able to wrestle the gun away from her. She was taken to jail and shortly after arriving, she asked to use the ladies room. Instead of heading into the bathroom, Grace dashed through the front door and escaped into the desert night.

Grace was found by a posse the next day. She was crouched

between two boulders, trying to hide from the authorities. Somehow, in the dark, she had made it fifteen miles through the desert, a landscape teeming with deadly snakes, scorpions and dangerous rocks and cliffs.

Her trial attracted a lot of attention, and many women came to see it, curious to know if she would get off after killing her husband. The jury wasn't out long, and they convicted Grace Nusser of murder, sentencing her to life in prison. She spent three years in prison before being committed to a state mental hospital in Reno where she died soon after.

The echo of Grace's murderous act still plays out in Boulder City. Local legend says that at times, late at night, a gunshot can be heard ringing out in the night, even though no one in town has fired a gun. Many believe it's the ghostly sound of the fatal gunshot that killed George that night in 1937.

But it isn't the only manifestation of the murder. To this day, there are claims that the bloody body of George Nusser, partially covered in a white sheet, appears in his old house. Perhaps it's an impression of the traumatic event, or perhaps it's the phantom of George, looking for his killer.

A Murderous Affair

The Hoover Dam

Dam Ghosts

First off, let's clarify the name of Southern Nevada's big dam. If you spend much time in the area, you're likely to hear it called both Boulder Dam and Hoover Dam. In bills passed by Congress to authorize the dam's construction, the project was referred to as Hoover Dam, a nod to then President Herbert Hoover. However, Hoover lost his reelection bid to Democrat Franklin Roosevelt, whose administration promptly renamed the project Boulder Dam. In 1947, Congress restored the original designation Hoover Dam, and it remains the official name. In modern times, Hoover Dam and Boulder Dam are used interchangeably.

The construction of the dam was an engineering marvel for its time. Many of the techniques used were largely unproven. Lake Mead was created because of the dam, and it is the largest reservoir in the United States—by volume, and when it's full, that is.

The construction project itself was major one that employed thousands of workers. The project was awarded to Six Companies, Inc. and President Hoover ordered construction to begin in 1931. Most of the work was completed by 1935, and the dam was officially turned over to the government in March 1936.

The dam is a big tourist attraction, pulling in over one million visitors a year who come to marvel at the sight of the massive engineering feat and take the dam tour.

Popular lore states that many men fell into the massive concrete walls and were unable to escape, effectively being buried alive. So, one of the first things many visitors want to know is—How many men were buried in the massive walls of the structure? The answer—None!

Despite how often the tale is repeated, there are no bodies in the structure of the dam. This isn't to say that men didn't die during construction of the site; in fact, many did. Official numbers list 96 deaths, though even this is disputed and often listed as high as 112. The discrepancy is in how the deaths are connected to the site, with the higher number noted as being deaths "associated with the construction of the dam."

Work on the dam was hard and dangerous, and the desert heat, with temperatures that can easily soar over 100 degrees, was challenging, especially for those who had moved from colder climates.

On December 20, 1922, J.G. Tierney was on a barge in the Colorado River. Tierney was an employee with the United States Bureau of Reclamation and was part of a geological survey team gathering information for a potential dam on the river. Specifically, they were scouting for the optimum location to build the dam. The trip was a tragic one for Tierney who drowned in the river's waters during a flash flood. In a creepy twist of fate, Tierney died near the spot where the Hoover Dam would eventually be built.

Exactly thirteen years later—December 20, 1935—another man died near the same spot. This time the victim fell from an intake tower at Hoover Dam. His name was Patrick W. Tierney. He was an electrician's helper and the son of the J.G.Tierney. The strange fate of the two Tierney men and their deaths is one of the weirdest incidents in the history of the Dam, and they are often noted as the first and last men to lose their lives in conjunction with the construction of the dam.

Of the ninety-six official deaths at the site, all the bodies were recovered and given proper burials, but some of their spirits may still linger.

One ghost reported at the dam is believed to be that of a worker who died in the 1930s. Several witnesses have spotted his apparition near the generators. He's described as wearing work clothes and an old hard hat. No one has reported any interaction with the spirit, so the manifestation could be another example of residual energy, the phantom impression of a deceased man still going about his daily work routine.

Other people say they've heard a voice calling to them in the dam's elevator. Some think it's the voice of a different man who perished at the site, one who slipped over a railing and fell to his death in 1983. He's also thought to be the same spirit that witnesses have spotted "walking his rounds" at the dam, continuing, even in the afterlife, to make sure everything is running properly and efficiently.

There are also numerous reports of shadow figures being seen around the dam. Shadow figures are exactly what they sound like—human figures that look like the shadows of men, yet move in a conscious, independent manner. If it sounds creepy, it usually is. People who encounter shadow figures are often frightened by the experience.

Phantoms and shadow figures are reportedly seen around Hoover Dam

Others claim they've seen the ghost of a woman walking around the dam. She turns up around sunrise and appears very somber. One woman who spotted the spirit felt sure it was the ghost of a woman who had committed suicide at the dam. It's certainly possible. In years past, there was a serious issue with people committing, or attempting to commit, suicide by jumping off the dam and into the waters below—a fatal fall from such a great height.

A phantom car has also been seen speeding across the dam. Those who have witnessed it say it's a vehicle from the 1950s. The car races along but fades into nothingness before it gets too close to the witness.

It's not just human spirits that hover around the dam. One of the ghosts most frequently spotted is that of a dog.

According to the story, during the construction of the dam, a little black dog showed up one day. Lost or abandoned, the dog found companionship among the dam workers who quickly became fond of him. The dog became a mascot for the project, and each morning, men would stop and greet him, giving him a pat on the head and sometimes a treat. Although times were tough for everyone, the little dog's food and water bowls were always full.

For his part, the little dog would often warn people when there was danger at the site. Somehow, it sensed when the men were in trouble. The dog was very devoted to the crew and would spend his days running to and from the damsite, visiting the various work areas.

But tragedy struck one day when a truck under which the dog was sleeping rolled over him and killed him. The men were heartbroken at the loss of the little dog. They gave him a burial that day and a bronze plaque was later placed to honor the dam workers' mascot. The animal is fondly remembered as "Nobody's Dog and Everybody's Dog."

The Hoover Dam construction crew's mascot was found as a puppy by workers at the construction camp. This dog traveled to and from the damsite with them and spent his days visiting the many work areas. On February 21, 1941, the life of this devoted animal came to an end when a truck under which he was sleeping rolled over him. The grave below was completed by workers later that same day.

A memorial plaque was erected to honor a devoted dog.

The phantom of the little black dog has been reported many times around the dam. Witnesses have spotted him running about the site and some say they've even called out to him and gotten his attention, but he fades away into thin air.

Others have heard the friendly barking of a dog at the site, even though no pets are allowed on the dam for safety reasons.

It should come as no surprise that people have speculated that the mob once tossed bodies off the dam and into the waters below, though whether this is truth or fanciful fiction is hard to say.

It is known that some early deaths at the site were caused by noxious gases, though these deaths were officially listed as "pneumonia" in order to limit liability. Still, if we add this number to the official death count, then the total begins to rise. And there's yet another factor—suicide. The dam was once a popular site for those committing, or attempting to commit, suicide, so much so that the top of the dam was put off limits to make it less appealing for those wishing to end their mortal existence.

No one is exactly sure why the dam was popular among those wanting to end their lives. Perhaps it's the spot's massive height—official records state that the dam is 726.4 feet—or perhaps it's the close proximity to Las Vegas, an intense city that changes many lives. In the past, those who lost their fortunes at the city's gambling tables may have taken their final breath before jumping off the top of the dam.

One old timer told me that he was sure there were people who had died in this fashion yet were listed simply as "missing." Such lost and desperate souls may have left a ghostly impression on the site, and it makes one wonder exactly how many people have died at the Hoover Dam throughout its history.

One young couple told me that they were at the dam late one evening in 2017. It was still light out, though the sun was quickly going down. There weren't many other people at the site and the couple was walking along casually. They noticed a woman coming towards them in an "old fashioned dress." The woman was alone and she, too, was walking calmly—that is, until she turned and suddenly leapt over the side of the dam. The terrified couple quickly looked out over the side, but there was nothing there. The female witness said that the woman seemed to jump up into the air and vanish. The witnesses believed they had seen the impression of a past event. As the man reported:

"I believe that we saw something from another time, a long time ago. It must have been some poor woman who wanted to end things and jumped off the dam."

Whatever the case, the Hoover Dam is a site rich in history and a statement of what humans can accomplish. It's listed on the National Register of Historic Places, is recognized as a National Civil Engineering Landmark, and is designated as a National Historic Landmark.

Aerial view of Hoover Dam

Hoover Dam Conspiracies

Over the years a lot of conspiracy theories have become attached to the Hoover Dam. Perhaps it's due to the structure's proximity to Las Vegas, or perhaps it's because the dam is such a massive, imposing piece of engineering. Whatever the case, the theories are at the least…interesting.

Early tales of purported bodies buried in the walls of the dam are nothing in comparison to some of the grand conspiracies that have cropped up in recent years. One of the zaniest theories was inspired by an incident that took place in 2015.

On May 8 a giant image was projected onto the walls of the Hoover Dam—the image of a white goat standing over twin towers. The massive image was projected on the dam for a week, and it resulted in an entangled conspiracy involving the Illuminati, the coming end times, and the rebirth of the Anti-Christ!

Conspiracy theorists quickly pointed out several things about the image. First, it was noted that the goat was standing over twin towers, something they believe harkened back to the terrible events of 9/11. The image, they believed, was an indication that another iconic structure in American was going to be destroyed. It was further noted that the goat was a stand-in for the satanic Baphomet, the goat headed figure used by the church of Satan and other similar groups.

It was also suggested that the projection of the goat was part of a large, satanic ritual that was unfolding right under everyone's noses, and, furthermore, it was a sign that the Anti-Christ himself was about to be summoned or reborn at the spot.

Some even claim that the dam itself resembles the throne of Satan, though how exactly anyone would know this is a mystery in itself.

Everyone waited with bated breath for the event. Well, not really. As it turned out, the explanation was fairly mundane.

Officials reported that a new projection system was being tested—the largest one in the world at the time—and the dam was being used as a screen. Employees conducting the test needed an image to use as part of their test. It just so happened that those conducting the tests were huge fans of FC Koln, a German soccer club, a team whose logo is—you guessed it—a goat standing over twin towers.

The goat projection came and went, and the devil didn't appear, but there have been plenty of other purported satanic connections to the Hoover Dam.

Another theory that cropped up involves the United States' fifty-dollar bill. Purportedly, folding the bill in a unique way—into a pentagram—reveals a hidden image, one that predicts the end of the Hoover Dam. The image shows the dam surrounded by four obelisks that the conspiracy minded say represents the number 11:11 and the destruction of the dam.

Yet another theory claims that the CERN Hadron Collider will be used to open a portal through which a horde of demons will enter the earth. The portal will be—you guessed it—right where the Hoover Dam is now.

Of course, Las Vegas has long been known as "Sin City" so, combined with the area's intense summer heat, perhaps it shouldn't be surprising that there are those who believe the gates of hell are going to open in the area.

Most locals who hear about the theories get a chuckle from them and believe they're absurd. The whole area, they say, just attracts the weird and unusual.

Boulder Beach
Lake Mead

National Park Service
U.S. Department of Interior
National Recreation Area

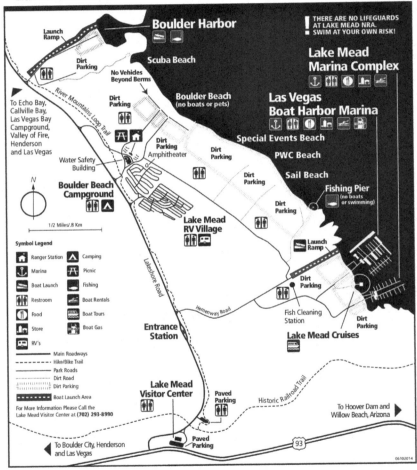

! THERE ARE NO LIFEGUARDS AT LAKE MEAD NRA. SWIM AT YOUR OWN RISK!

Boulder Harbor

Scuba Beach

Lake Mead Marina Complex

Launch Ramp

Dirt Parking

No Vehicles Beyond Berms

Boulder Beach (no boats or pets)

Dirt Parking

Las Vegas Boat Harbor Marina

To Echo Bay, Callville Bay, Las Vegas Bay Campground, Valley of Fire, Henderson and Las Vegas

River Mountains Loop Trail

Dirt Parking

Amphitheater

Dirt Parking

Special Events Beach

Dirt Parking

PWC Beach

Water Safety Building

Sail Beach

Dirt Parking

Fishing Pier (no boats or swimming)

N

Boulder Beach Campground

Dirt Parking

Lake Mead RV Village

Dirt Parking

Launch Ramp

1/2 Miles/.8 Km

Symbol Legend

Lakeshore Road

Dirt Parking

🏠 Ranger Station   ⛺ Camping
⚓ Marina   🌲 Picnic
🚤 Boat Launch   🎣 Fishing
🚻 Restroom   🚣 Boat Rentals
🍴 Food   🚢 Boat Tours
🏪 Store   ⛽ Boat Gas
🚐 RV's

Hemenway Road

Fish Cleaning Station

Dirt Parking

Lake Mead Cruises

Main Roadways
Hike/Bike Trail
Park Roads
Dirt Road
Dirt Parking
Boat Launch Area

For More Information Please Call the
Lake Mead Visitor Center at **(702) 293-8990**

Entrance Station

Lake Mead Visitor Center

Paved Parking

Historic Railroad Trail

To Hoover Dam and Willow Beach, Arizona ▶

Paved Parking

◀ **To Boulder City, Henderson and Las Vegas**

93

06102014

Lake Mead

Lake Mead is a large reservoir that was formed by the creation of the Hoover Dam. It provides fresh water to Nevada, Arizona and California, and is the largest reservoir in the United States in terms of water capacity.

The lake was named after Elwood Mead, commissioner of the U. S. Bureau of Reclamation from 1924 to 1936, the years that the Hoover Dam was built.

The lake sparkles like a jewel in the desert sun and it's a popular spot for recreational activities. Fishing, boating and other water sports, as well as other outdoor activities, are a big draw at the lake. Millions of people visit the area each year. They come to enjoy the unique desert oasis. Few of them know about the strange things that lie at the bottom of the lake.

On the afternoon of May 16, 1943, Howard Hughes conducted a test flight of an experimental seaplane at Lake Mead. The craft lifted into the air but suddenly nosedived and crashed into the water. The aircraft's propellor snapped off and went into the plane where it hit mechanic Richard Felt, slicing his head. The propeller embedded itself into the plane and knocked another man, William "Ceco" Cline, into the lake. Cline was an inspector for the Civil Aeronautics Administration. Cline was lost in the water, dead from the blow he took or from drowning or a combination of the two.

Howard Hughes, his co-pilot Richard Felt, and another engineer all escaped before the plane sank into the water. The men were soon rescued but Felt succumbed to his injuries two days later and passed away. Hughes received a severe blow to his head and spent some time at the Boulder Dam Hotel while he recovered. Hughes's plane was later recovered, though the body of William Cline was never found.

When the waters rushed in and filled Lake Mead, it wasn't just empty desert that was submerged. Bonelli's Ferry, a river crossing between Nevada and Arizona, was sent beneath the water, as were the river landings of Callville and Rioville. Even more notable, the historic town of St. Thomas was covered by the creation of the lake.

St. Thomas was an early Mormon settlement founded in 1865. At the time the dam was built, St. Thomas had a population of around two thousand people.

By the time the waters rushed in, most of the residents had evacuated, with many relocating to the nearby town of Overton. A handful of people held out until the last possible moment, with the final resident leaving in 1938 as the water flooded into his home.

A lot of St. Thomas was left behind. Buildings still stood; items that couldn't be easily moved were abandoned; and, according to some legends, at least some of the dead were left behind. Of course, none of the residents of the small community wanted to leave their deceased friends and relatives behind to be submerged beneath the incoming waters, and they made every effort to disinter the bodies and relocate them to Overton.

The ruins of St. Thomas

Of course, the unsettling question lingers: were they able to move them all? And even if they were all relocated, is it ever a good idea to disturb the dead?

When the water levels of the lake fall during periods of drought, the remnants of St. Thomas can be seen rising like an eerie specter out of the water. Witnesses say that during these times, a ghostly young woman is seen walking among the ruins.

The town of St. Thomas isn't the only odd thing at the bottom of the big southern Nevada lake. There's also an airplane! Specifically, a B-29 Superfortress from World War Two. The plane crashed into the water on July 21, 1948. All five men on board survived, but the plane went to its watery grave and has lain there ever since, a home for the lake's aquatic creatures.

And speaking of water creatures, some of the ones living in Lake Mead may be of considerable size. According to the Nevada Department of Wildlife, both bullhead and channel catfish have been verified in the lake. Catfish can reach monstrous proportions and there's no telling how big those living in the lake are, but some people have claimed to have seen massive specimens. Of course, they always seem to be the ones that got away!

Stranger than catfish are the rumors of other unusual animals living in the lake. Sometimes the stories are simply folklore. In the 1970s and 1980s, tales of sharks in the lake made the rounds and it was claimed that the finned terrors had attacked some boaters. Considering that the hit movie *Jaws* came out in 1975, it's likely that shark fever resulted in the stories. There's no evidence that indicated that sharks have graced the waters of Lake Mead.

A report from 2013 states that someone witnessed a man releasing alligators into the lake. No one has ever reported being attacked by a gator at the lake, and if the account is true, it was most likely an exotic pet that was being abandoned. State wildlife officials note that people frequently abandon exotic pets when the animals grow too large or become difficult to deal with. Why someone would choose to release such a dangerous animal into a recreational lake is, of course, an entirely different puzzle.

The stories are part and parcel of the bevy of odd tales that have sprung up about the lake over the years. By some accounts, there are piles of casino chips worth thousands of dollars down in the water, and of course, there are rumors of mob murder victims having been tossed into Lake Mead. Whether or not there's any truth to that, we'll never know—unless something surfaces, that is. We do know that people have died at the lake over the years. In fact, in 2017, the Lake Mead National Recreation Area was named the "deadliest park in America." The dubious honor was bestowed on the park by *Outside* magazine, who reported that Lake Mead had an average of 25 deaths each year, and that in the previous decade there had been 254 deaths at the site. Mead was well ahead of the next most dangerous park—California's Yosemite, which had 150 deaths.

According to the report, causes of death at Lake Mead ranged from suicide to accidental drowning, but Mead also registered a number of homicides, more than any other national park at the time of the research.

Perhaps the lake's dangers could account for some of the restless spirits that seem to be present. One young man told me that he had an unnerving experience at the lake one day. He had hung out with some friends who had all left earlier, but he had stayed behind, relaxing, and reading a book. The sun was just starting to go down and the man was picking up his things, preparing to leave, when he heard a blood curdling scream.

"It was a woman screaming, and it was right there beside me. I grew up with several sisters, and they screamed in my ear plenty of times. It was just like that. I got the coldest chill that rushed over me. There was NO ONE in sight. I left as quick as I could."

There are other spirits at the lake that aren't as disturbing. People have spotted the phantom of a young man who runs up out of the water. He appears happy as if he's having a wonderful time, but once he reaches the lake's shore, he disappears, leaving witnesses stunned and puzzled over what they saw with their own eyes.

A ghostly couple from another time has been seen by several witnesses. They appear fully clothed in dress that appears to be from early pioneer days. Witnesses say the pair are most often seen at night. They come strolling out of the darkness, talking to each other and walking calmly. As witnesses watch, the couple walks into the water where they vanish. Perhaps they're trying to get home to St. Thomas.

Others who have spent time around the lake claim to have heard Native American voices and chanting and are convinced that the spirits of long-lost tribal people haunt the land.

There are even ghosts that travel the surface of Lake Mead. There's a paddle boat called the Desert Princess that takes people on tours around the lake and the boat has a resident spirit, a female ghost known as Sally.

Sally is said to be the spirit of a tourist who fell down the stairs, hit her head, and died shortly afterwards. She is a bit of a trickster and likes to turn the volume up on music, unplug things, and cause general low-key mischief.

There's another afterlife connection of sorts regarding the Desert Princess. Although it's illegal, a lot of people ask their loved ones to dump their cremated remains into Lake Mead.

The easiest way to accomplish this is, of course, from a boat while on the lake. As a result, hoping to honor the wishes of the dead, many people decide to skirt the law and quietly carry the ashes of the deceased with them during their outings on the paddleboat. But there's a bit of an issue—there's a ledge around the boat and most of the ashes end up getting stuck there. So, the ship is literally lined with the ashes of departed souls

Lake Mead

Lake Mead

A Lost Haunt

One location in Boulder City that was reportedly haunted is now gone. The Boulder City Hospital once sat atop a hill overlooking Lake Mead.

The hospital originally opened in 1931 and was built to care for men who had fallen sick or gotten injured while working on the Hoover Dam. Worker's wives and children weren't treated at the hospital—they had to travel to Las Vegas for medical help. The hospital remained in service until work on the dam was completed. In 1938 the National Park Service took control of the hospital building and converted it into a museum. The building's stint as a museum was short lived, and the Park Service moved out in 1941.

In 1943 the U.S. Public Health Service took the building over and used it for soldiers who were injured while fighting in World War II.

In 1949 the building fell under the control of another government agency—the Bureau of Reclamation. They held onto it until 1954.

After that, the old hospital sat abandoned for years until the Episcopalian Sisters of Charity purchased it in 1976. The order transformed the building into a facility called the Wellsprings Retreat House. The building operated as a retreat center until 2009 when it was listed for sale with a whopping $1.5 million dollar price tag. The building didn't sell until 2015 when developer Randolph Schams purchased it for $550,000, well below the original asking price.

Schams planned to demolish the building and put in a subdivision. The plan was not well received by citizens of Boulder City. After all, the historic building had been placed on the National Register of Historic Places in 1982, and it was a notable part of the city's history.

Despite a citizen-organized fight against demolition, the city council voted to allow Schams to move forward with his plan and the hospital was torn down.

During the years the building sat abandoned, it gained a local reputation for being haunted. Reports included strange moaning sounds, phantom footsteps, and sightings of shadow figures. Other people claimed to have seen apparitions inside the building.

One man told me he'd been inside the old hospital a year prior to its demolition. He said that he and a friend wanted to conduct their own ghost hunt like they'd seen on television. They carried a camera and recorder with them to the site. Once inside, they heard what sounded like footsteps following them through the building. Curiously, they found it impossible to capture the footsteps on their digital recorder. As he recalls:

"Footsteps followed us all around inside the building but every time we turned on the recorder they would stop. We tried everything we could think of. And it wasn't any kind of echo of our steps either. There were two of us and we only heard one set of footsteps following us. Plus, we tried to catch them by walking slowly and turning the recorder on as we walked, but again, as soon as the record button was hit, the footsteps stopped. At one point, we ran down a hallway and stopped suddenly. We heard the steps running behind us as if whatever it was wanted to catch up with us."

Another witness named Robert told me that he'd seen an apparition in one of the building's windows. He said the incident occurred in 2016. Thinking the building was going to be torn down, the man and a friend went to explore the site. They arrived late at night and stood outside, considering whether or not to go in. Robert told me he was cautious because he was afraid of being arrested for trespassing on the property.

Robert's companion was busy changing the batteries in a flashlight so while he waited, Robert stood looking closely at the building. He noticed something odd in one of the second story windows. He reports:

"It was a woman standing at one of the windows. She was wearing a white top of some kind and at first, I thought 'oh, there's someone else inside,' but she just…vanished. I caught my breath and stepped back. My friend asked what was wrong and all I could say was, 'I'm not going in there.' We left and that was it, I never went back up to the place."

I asked Robert if, in hindsight, he thought he'd seen a ghost or if it had been a trick of the mind because of his apprehension.

"I've thought about that myself. Part of me really thinks it was a ghost. Maybe it was the ghost of a nurse or someone who died there. But maybe I was just seeing into the past somehow, to a time when the place was a hospital. There were no other cars around and she didn't look like a homeless person, plus, the way she vanished. I can't explain it, it's still a mystery for me."

Who or what was in the old hospital building? Was it inhabited by the spirits of those who spent time there, or was it simply a storehouse of energy that gave off impressions of the past for those sensitive enough to detect them?

Since the structure has been torn down, we may never know. Then again, perhaps the new buildings constructed on the site will have their own haunts to report.

The Boulder Dam Hotel

On December 15, 1933, a grand opening gala was held for the new Boulder Dam Hotel. The place was a hit, according to the area newspaper, the *Las Vegas Evening Review-Journal*, which stated:

"The hotel compares in beauty with any famous hotels along the coast and has the advantage of smallness."

Small it was, especially in comparison to modern mega hotels. Even today, the Boulder Dam Hotel only has twenty-two rooms. It sits in the middle of town on Arizona Street and has long been a central point of the city.

Foregoing the popular art deco style that dominated buildings of the period, original builder Paul Stewart "Jim" Webb elected to build the hotel in a Colonial Revival style.

Webb and his business partner, Raymond Spilsbury, had made their fortunes in real estate in southern California. With the creation of the "government town" of Boulder City, and the massive dam project, the writing was on the wall—there was money to be made in southern Nevada.

The hotel was built to accommodate tourists and visitors coming to marvel at the massive construction project. And come they did. Many of the period's celebrities and elite stayed at the hotel in its heyday. Among them, actors Boris Karloff, Shirley Temple, Bette Davis, and Henry Fonda. American business magnate Cornelius Vanderbilt stayed at the hotel on his honeymoon, The Duchess of Westminster slept at the hotel, as did the Maharaja and Maharani of Indore, India, and Cardinal Pascelli, the man who would later become Pope Pius XII. In short, the guest list is a veritable historic who's who.

Confident of the hotel's success, Webb soon added more

rooms and a large dining room to the facility, but it wasn't long before things went awry. Webb's other business ventures didn't fare well and as a result, he let the hotel languish. He simply didn't have the money to spend on upkeep and maintenance.

The real issue came in 1941. With World War II underway, the federal government closed the dam to visitors due to concerns over possible terrorist attacks.

Without its main attraction open, the hotel's business began to fall. Raymond Spilsbury bought Webb out and took the hotel over. He started making improvements and returned the business to a profitable state. Spilsbury may have made the hotel successful again, but a strange fate was in store for him. In January 1945 the businessman disappeared. On January 23 the *Boulder City News* reported that his hat and dress coat were found near Eldorado Canyon. The items were neatly folded and had a rock placed on top to keep them from blowing away. Spilsbury's fate was unknown and would remain so for over a month.

On February 27 the *Boulder City News* announced that a body had been discovered in the water at the edge of the Colorado River eight miles downstream from Spilsbury's last known location. When the body was retrieved, it was confirmed to be that of Raymond Spilsbury. When law enforcement officers pull the body from the water, they discovered that the man's feet had been bound with his own belt, and his pockets had been filled with rocks.

The coroner ruled Spilsbury's death a suicide.

In the following years, the fortunes of the Boulder Dam Hotel were up and down. It went through numerous owners and bankruptcies and was even closed for a time. In the 1960s, it served as a retirement home for the elderly.

The Boulder Dam Hotel was added to the National Register of Historic Places in 1982, but it didn't help the difficult times the business went through. Things had grown worse over the years and at one point the hotel was even condemned. Fortunately, locals banded together and formed the "Friends of the Hotel" group in 1993. Extensive renovations were started and in 2005 the hotel was taken over by the Boulder City Museum and Historical Association with the goal of restoring the hotel as a central part of the city and its history and culture.

The historic Boulder Dam Hotel

The hotel also houses the Boulder City/Hoover Dam Museum, a detailed and educational museum that shows the history of the city and the dam.

Like many historic properties, the Boulder Dam Hotel has gained a reputation over the years for having some resident ghosts. Unlike many locations, however, the hotel does not try to capitalize on the spirits. In fact, the hotel actively discourages any idea that the hotel is haunted. Naturally, this only serves to make some people all the more curious about any potential hauntings at the property, and despite the assertion of some, there are stories that continue to circulate.

Reportedly, at one time, a maid was cleaning a room and had a weird experience. She had made the bed and gone to the hallway to retrieve something from her housekeeping cart. When she walked back into the room, there was an imprint on the freshly made bed as if someone had sat down on it, yet, there was no one in sight! To say the least, it gave her a chill.

According to a desk clerk I spoke to during one of my stays at the property, there have never been any reported murders or strange deaths at the hotel. He assured me that rumors of ghosts in the building were "absolutely not true."

The man wasn't rude about the topic, but he was quite adamant about his statement and told me that it was the stance of the hotel managers and owners. Still, there are other opinions.

A woman I spoke with in town was a former employee of the hotel, and she believes there are a few ghosts running about at the property.

"Rooms 209 and 219 always gave me the creeps. I always felt like someone else was in the room with me, or that I was being watched," she told me.

The woman was careful to tell me that it was her experience and her belief, a further emphasis on the town's stark differences in opinion regarding hauntings at the Boulder Dam Hotel.

The clerk I spoke with told me that he believed the entire basis of hauntings at the hotel came from the visit of a psychic who was at the property in the 1980s. Her impressions appeared as the final chapter in the 1993 book *Midnight on Arizona Street: The Secret Life of the Boulder Dam Hotel* by Dennis McBride.

McBride was a Boulder City historian who worked at the facility. Years ago, while working at the hotel museum, he had an encounter with a ghost. At the time, McBride was a collections specialist. He was working alone one evening and everything was quiet. McBride happened to look up and was astonished to see a man standing in the doorway. He described the man as dark, mustached, and visible only from the waist up. Clearly it was not a living human being!

McBride didn't sense any malevolence from the man. More than anything, the spirit seemed to be curious about what McBride was doing.

In his book, McBride states that ghost stories had long been associated with the hotel:

"There have been reports of spirit activity at the Boulder

Dam Hotel for years. Some of the stories involve mundane supernatural mischief, like objects disappearing and reappearing in unlikely places. Other stories are too outrageous to be believed: floating heads and bleeding walls."

McBride's personal encounter is an interesting one. Was it the phantom of someone who had worked on the Hoover Dam? Perhaps a possession of the man's had ended up in the museum collection, or perhaps it was just a wandering spirit not connected to the hotel or museum at all. Whatever the case, the incident made McBride curious enough to contact a psychic to do a reading on the hotel's past and any potential ghosts.

With the help of a friend, McBride brought in well-known psychic Patsy Welding. Welding arrived on the night of August 16, 1980, and spent two hours walking around the hotel, relaying her impressions of the spirits she detected inside.

According to Welding, there were ghosts all over the hotel. Spirits inside ranged from a very sad woman on the verge of suicide in room 219, to a group of hard drinkers on the second floor of the southeast wing.

Welding was particularly disturbed by the hotel's basement, and she refused to enter the area, telling McBride that "It's as though something waits there."

McBride writes that he was aware of incidents that others had reported about the basement:

"People who've spent time in the basement have felt uneasy, panicky, watched. Workers have fled the basement claiming they felt a hand reach up from the floor to grab their ankles."

The psychic believed that someone had been murdered in the basement of the hotel, and she insisted that the energy was dark and unsettled. McBride notes that the murder victim's spirit may have been seen in the hotel, at least by one witness:

"A desk clerk from the early 1980s claims to have several times been confronted in the lobby by the partial manifestation of a rough-looking man whose face is masked in blood. He seemed anxious and distracted and his lips moved as though he were trying to speak."

There haven't been any such dramatic reports from the hotel in decades, and one wonders what may have happened to the disturbed spirits if indeed they were ever present. Did they find peace or move on? Or was the psychic way off base with her purported impressions?

Ghost stories that are based on singular accounts are always a mixed bag and some people don't put stock in psychic information at all.

There are still ghostly tales about the hotel, of course, but they are subdued, and, some would say, even pleasant. The most common report in recent years is the sound of phantom piano music coming from the lobby. Some people even recognize the tune, inevitably a song from a time long past. Sometimes there's a strong smell of cigar smoke in the lobby, even though no smoking is allowed inside.

It's not hard to have the sense of spirits of the past in the hotel's lobby. When the building was renovated—a project that took over two million dollars and several years to complete— great care was taken to retain the original beauty of the lobby. It's decorated in rich, dark colors, there's an oversized fireplace, and a grand piano. Small groupings of classic chairs and settees are spread about and are perfect for conversations and drinks. A framed, sepia-toned photograph of the original lobby shows just how much today's version resembles the past.

Some people have eerie feelings in the museum while they're wandering through the exhibits and learning about the history of the dam from its inception to completion and opening. The oral histories, photographs, maps, and interactive displays tell the story and relate the human toll the dam took on workers and their families, and this alone gives one a glimpse of the past and a sense of haunting memories of a different time in history.

Perhaps there are spirits in the hotel, open to communicating with those who believe or who are sensitive to such things. One person who had spent a lot of time in the hotel told me that strange incidents do occur there, things that simply couldn't

be explained by logical means: items that move about on their own, cold spots, doors that open and close on their own, and phantom knocks at rooms late at night when the hallways are empty.

Other people claim that whispered voices are heard at times when no one else is present. There may be spirits in the hotel that will be forever unknown, lost to the past, or these could be spirits that visitors bring with them.

If you're brave enough to venture down into the basement, it's now home to a speakeasy called Cleveland's Lounge. Somehow, it seems fitting and in keeping with the unique hotel and it gives one the opportunity to at least experience some spirits at the Boulder Dam Hotel, albeit not of the ghostly kind.

At the least, the ghosts of the past, of the building, the city, and its storied history, do indeed linger at the Boulder Dam Hotel. Stay if you can, visit the museum, enjoy the ambiance, and keep your mind and eyes open. You just never know how shades of the past may show up.

The Boulder Theater circa 1932

Boulder Theater

When it was built in 1932, the Boulder Theater was the largest theater in Nevada, and when it opened its doors it was the only building in Boulder City with air conditioning. No doubt, this made it even more attractive for those seeking both an evening's entertainment and a break from the desert heat.

On New Year's Eve, 1934, the theater hosted the world premiere of the film *Silver Streak*, starring Charles Starrett and Sally Blane. The premier was a star-studded event with many of Hollywood's elite on hand. The movie itself wasn't very successful, but the Boulder Theater was, and for years, the house was frequently packed with people anxious to see filmland's newest releases.

By the 1990s, the small theater was unable to compete with the large megaplex movie screens that had sprung up around the valley and it closed its doors. But it wasn't the end for the historic building. In 1998, Desi Arnaz Jr., son of famous actors Desi Arnaz and Lucille Ball, stepped in. Desi and his wife, Amy, purchased the Boulder Theater and took it over for use as the center for their non-profit children's ballet company, the Boulder City Ballet Company. The pair did a major renovation on the theater to bring it up to code while keeping a classic, 1930s style.

It should come as no surprise that there are reports of ghostly activity at the historic site. After all, theaters are places of high energy and lots of emotion. Years of performances and responsive audiences can leave an impression on such places and result in residual hauntings. (A residual haunting is a "recording" of an event that replays under certain conditions.)

At least one famous ghost, or an echo of his presence, reportedly hangs out at the Boulder Theater—the great humorist, cowboy, and actor—Will Rogers.

Rogers performed on the theater's stage in 1935, not long before he died in a tragic plane crash. Rogers was only fifty-five at the time of his passing, and his death was a shock to the nation who adored his wit and charm.

Some swear they've heard the ghostly voice of Rogers coming from the stage at the Boulder Theater. His voice is often followed by phantom laughter that rings out from the audience, a statement perhaps on the timeless humor and charisma he was reputed to have.

Most likely, the voice of Will Rogers in the Boulder Theater is an example of a residual haunting rather than the conscious presence of the man himself. Nevertheless, in a curious way, it helps carry on his memory.

Another spirit that reportedly manifests in the theater seems to be a bit more interactive.

Reports say that a tap dance teacher once had a chilling experience in the building one night while he was rehearsing.

*Some believe the spirit of Will Rogers
lingers at the Boulder Theater*

The man was alone on stage when the air around him became ice cold. The man stopped and started searching for the source of the cold breeze when someone, or rather, something, unseen gently tapped him on the shoulder.

The startling experience left the man convinced that the theater is haunted, and after his brush with the phantom, the teacher refused to be in the building alone after dark.

The spirit may be that of a man who reportedly passed away in the theater in the 1940s. Legend says the man died of a heart attack while attending a movie. His sudden passing may have left his spirit confused and connected to the last place he visited. His ghost may be the same one that other people have spotted in the building over the years. According to some reports, the man appears as a faint apparition that fades away. He's been seen walking around in the theater, though no one has communicated with him or gotten a clear description of his features.

One witness told me that she was working in the theater one day when she was startled to see someone sitting in one of the seats near the front. She was startled because she knew that all the doors were locked, and she believed she was alone in the building.

The man was gray haired and was lying back in the seat as if he had dozed off. The woman assumed that a homeless person had wandered in, and she walked cautiously down the aisle toward him, calling out to wake him up. When she had almost reached the aisle where he was sitting, the figure faded away. The witness stood stunned and suddenly realized she had seen a ghost.

In recent years, the Boulder Theater has hosted the "Dam Short Film Festival," an annual event that has brought the location back full circle to its original purpose. The theater also plays host to performing artists and a dance company, making it a cornerstone of Boulder City's arts community.

The Boulder Theater is part of the Boulder City Historic District and is located at 1225 Arizona Street.

Boulder Theater

The Boulder Pet Cemetery

Human spirits aren't the only ghosts wandering around the Boulder City area. We've already discussed the phantom dog at Hoover Dam, but there are more ghosts of the animal kind. Just outside of town is a location where many locals have been interring their deceased pets for years and according to some, there are some animal spirits still lingering about at the site.

It's commonly known as the Boulder Pet Cemetery, though since it's an "unofficial" site, it's known by other names as well, including Searchlight Road Pet Cemetery, The El Dorado Valley Pet Cemetery and the Marwood Doud Pet Cemetery.

Technically, it's never been legal for people to bury their pets on this patch of land, but it's been a long-standing tradition in the Las Vegas Valley, and, for the most part, officials seem to turn a blind eye to the practice.

Historians say the cemetery was started in the 1950s by a man named Emory Lockette. Lockette was a civil engineer and was looking for a way to make a few extra bucks. He started offering burial plots for deceased pets in an area of about three acres in size outside of Boulder City. No one seemed to take notice that Lockette was selling plots on government land. He charged between sixty and eighty dollars, and the cost included a plot and small wooden fences along the perimeter.

Eventually, the Bureau of Land Management stepped in and shut down Lockette's little enterprise, but by that time, the cemetery was a firm part of the community and locals continued to use it as a place of final rest for their deceased animal friends.

At one point, city officials put up a fence and posted signs to notify people that burials were not allowed on the land, but the signs were ignored, and the cemetery continued to grow.

There's a wide variety of markers at the cemetery. Some are simple wooden crosses with the animal's name written on, some are piles of stones, and others are more elaborate, professionally made headstones carved with the animal's name and birth and death years chiseled in.

Dennis McBride, director of the Nevada State Museum, told Fox News 5 that he visits the cemetery periodically and is impressed by the care that people have put into the graves:

"It's so personal the way these pets have been buried in ways that you're not allowed to in any kind of conventional cemetery. It's just folk art. Folk ways, that is very important, I think, and so I hope it stays that way, and I'll continue my visits and take pictures as the graves disappear back into the sand."

There's even a pet celebrity buried at the site. "Flash" was the son of Rin Tin Tin IV. Flash had a shot at stardom in the 1950s show, but a poor screen showing caused him to be replaced.

According to some local lore, the site had a more sinister side at one point—it was reputedly a dumping ground for those killed by the Las Vegas Mob. Such stories are merely fanciful rumors though. There's never been any evidence or indication that mafia victims or any other humans have been buried on the grounds. In truth, the location would not serve well for criminals to hide their victims. The desert soil erodes quickly, and the area is in a zone vulnerable to flash flooding.

Still, some who visit the cemetery find themselves overwhelmed with waves of sadness and intense emotion. Considering how many people feel about their animal companions, this should come as no surprise. At the least, such emotional intensity has likely left a strong impression on the cemetery.

But there are some who say the spirits of some animals still roam the site. There are reports of a ghostly golden lab that's seen wandering through the cemetery at night.

Even more frequent are the sightings of a large white cat. Numerous people have encountered the feline, felt it brush against their legs, and tried to pick up only to have it vanish before their eyes.

One woman spotted the cat and thought it was a stray or had been abandoned. She fully intended to rescue the cat and knelt down, calling to it. When it got close, she reached out to scoop it up, only to find that her hands passed through the animal, and it faded away.

Another person who visited the site told me that she heard what sounded like a small bell like a cat would have on its collar, jingling behind her as she walked around the graves.

Other witnesses have reported hearing a strange howling sound echoing around the cemetery at night. Are these simply residual energies of animals that have passed on to the next world, or are they conscious spirits hoping to stay connected to their former owners? Whatever the case, the great attachment that people feel toward their animals can be felt very distinctly at the cemetery.

Gary and Cindy Carlson published *Searchlight Road Pet Cemetery*, a book about the site and its many graves. The couple reports that they have documented around two thousand burials at the location.

"We found everything from lizards, snakes, cats, dogs, even horses and we found a few mules or donkeys."

At one point, there was a campaign to have the site recognized as a "legitimate" cemetery, but it never came to pass. In 1995, Boulder City purchased roughly 85,000 acres in the Eldorado Valley and designated it as Desert Tortoise Habitat. The city ordinance that covers the designation makes it illegal to bury remains on the land.

The Boulder Pet Cemetery is off the northbound side of U.S. 95, just south of Boulder City. It's somewhat difficult to find and locals seem to like it that way, but if you find yourself out at the site one quiet night, watch and listen closely, you just may have a phantom animal make its presence known.

The Boulder Pet Cemetery

*Tom Devlin's Monster Museum pays tribute
to decades of movie monsters*

Movie Monsters in Boulder City

Boris Karloff, famous for his role in Universal monster movies such as *The Mummy* and *Frankenstein*, lived in the Boulder Dam Hotel in 1946 so that he could establish Nevada residency. Karloff wanted a quick divorce from his fifth wife, Dorothy Stine, a woman who he said was "cruel to him."

Karloff even performed on stage at the Boulder Theater, but he didn't hang around too long. Right after his divorce, he married his sixth wife and headed for Hollywood to continue his movie career.

Movie monster star Boris Karloff spent time in Boulder City

But there are still monsters to be found in the small town. Right on Nevada Highway is a building with an amazing assortment of monster movie memorabilia—Tom Devlin's Monster Museum.

Tom Devlin loves monsters. Since 2001, he's worked in the field of makeup and special effects. But it's not just a job for Tom, it's his passion. His company 1313FX has provided creatures and makeup effects for over a hundred feature films.

Devlin became a fan favorite after appearing on SyFy's makeup themed contest show, "Face Off." Following his passion for monsters, Devlin decided to open a museum to highlight his collection. His goal is to educate the public about the art that he loves so much. The success of *Face Off* brought more attention to the field of monster makeup and effects, and Devlin thought it would be great to have a museum that highlights the history of the field.

As the museum's website states:

"Our mission is to preserve the art and history of special makeup effects. This gallery of Tom's art includes everything from screen used props and creature suits to custom pieces representing monsters throughout movie history."

Tom has worked on over a hundred films and has traveled around the country for gigs. His museum reflects the range of his interest in monsters and the place is constantly growing with new exhibits and pieces added on a regular basis.

There are screen used props from movies such as the Puppet Master franchise, creepy Chucky dolls and props from the films and much, much more. And don't worry, the classic monsters are present and accounted for, including Karloff's Frankenstein and the Mummy.

Area 51, UFOs, and the Alien Presence

If you're thinking about weird things in Nevada, the first thing that comes to mind is most likely UFOs. (Well, and Las Vegas, but we're talking about the paranormal, supernatural kind of weird.)

There's a good reason for the UFO connection of course; the region is home to the famous Area 51, or Groom Lake, a top-secret government installation rumored to hide UFOs, aliens, and all sorts of other strange things. Area 51 is the secret base that hasn't stayed very secret, at least in terms of public awareness of the base's existence.

Some people believe that Area 51 has, or at least once had—depending on opinion—wreckage from a crashed flying saucer retrieved from Roswell, New Mexico, in 1947.

Conspiracy theories have long run rampant about Area 51 and its potential harboring of aliens or at least alien technology. The idea that the base holds such secrets led to a strange, frenzied event in 2019 dubbed "Storm Area 51." It's exactly what it sounds like—a plan to gather around the base and invade it. The concept started as an internet-based idea and it soon trended on social media platforms, spreading like wildfire, and catching the attention of people around the world. The mainstream media helped, publishing stories that fueled the fire even more. Authorities grew concerned about the constantly growing number of people that were reportedly planning to show up and storm the base. Speculation ran wild that upwards of a million people were going to travel to the desert and rush onto Area 51. "They can't stop us all" was the event slogan.

It should be noted here that security is taken very seriously at Area 51. Armed personnel guard the perimeter and simply stepping over the line in the sand and onto the base is enough to lead to a rapid arrest by authorities, or worse. Guards commonly known as "cammo dudes" are reportedly authorized to use lethal force on anyone who intrudes onto the base's territory without authorization. Despite such threats, the wild idea continued to grow as the September date for storming the base approached.

Ultimately, only around 150 individuals showed up for the event and many of them were simply curious spectators who wanted to see what was going to happen. In the end, not much occurred and whatever mysteries are at Area 51 have held fast.

A warning sign posted at Area 51

Some people doubt that alien craft are buzzing the skies of Nevada and think that anomalous sightings are simply test aircraft being flown by U.S. pilots. Fingers are often pointed at Area 51 as the origin point for such test craft. From a logical perspective, it makes some sense. The vast, wide-open skies of the Nevada desert are certainly a good place for test flights, and if the government is building experimental aircraft at the base, they certainly wouldn't announce their work.

Still, rumors of aliens and extraterrestrial craft persist, and many believers insist that it's not just military aircraft soaring in the night skies of Nevada.

Perhaps the sightings are of extraterrestrial crafts and the aliens are stopping by in search of some writing implements. After all, the famous Fisher Space Pen was manufactured in Boulder City.

The pen was patented in 1965 and uses pressurized ink cartridges that allow it to write in a wide range of temperatures, on greasy paper, underwater, and even in zero gravity.

Prior to the invention of the pen, astronauts were using pencils, but graphite dust from pencil tips was a danger to onboard electronics. When the Fisher pen was created, (and after plenty of testing), NASA purchased Fisher pens for use on Apollo missions.

Many of those early pens are considered collectors' items. Apollo 17 astronaut Gene Cernan's pen was sold at a Heritage auction in 2008 for $23,900. A hefty sum for an ink pen!

But test craft and fancy ink pens aside, southern Nevada is rife with the alien motif. From the famous Extraterrestrial Highway to the Area 51 Alien Center and Alien Fresh Jerky (yeah, don't ask), the idea of aliens, at least the pop-culture version, seem to be everywhere.

But before we dismiss the idea as simple creative marketing and hype, let's consider an important factor—there's a long history of UFO sightings in the region.

Take, for instance, an impressive unidentified flying object report from the mid-1950s.

In mid-August 1956 a man named Edison F. Carpenter was sitting on the back porch of his home in Boulder City. It was 10:15 at night and Carpenter and his wife were enjoying the night when they saw something very strange in the sky— UFOs. Not just a singular craft, but five of them!

Carpenter wasn't just a run of the mill observer; he was a research technician for North American Aviation. The couple were facing south, the night was clear, and there was a gentle breeze breaking the desert heat. The UFOs appeared suddenly, flying in a partial V-Formation. Carpenter stated:

"Suddenly from directly overhead, they had come over the house from the north. We became aware of a group of slightly glowing objects as they flew to the south."

Carpenter, a trained observer, watched the craft closely and noted details:

"Their shape was perfectly round as viewed from below and they had a sort of phosphorescent glow (pinkish in color). The general shape must have been round and flat rather than round like a ball because as they drew away the shape was [oval] rather than [circular] as a ball would appear from any angle."

After the incident, Carpenter reported the sighting to the National Investigative Committee on Aerial Phenomena (NICAP). Regarding the movement of the craft, Carpenter further noted in his official report:

"They held the formation while in view and maintained a spacing of approximately one diameter between ships. This diameter was about the diameter of a cigarette cross-section held at arm's length. They crossed approximately 60 degrees of sky, from the time they came into view over our roof until I lost sight of them, in about six seconds. I'm quite sure of the time element because pistol shooting is a hobby of mine, and I've become accustomed to counting off ten to twenty seconds for rapid and timed fire."

Carpenter's sighting in Boulder City was a significant one, but he's certainly not the only person to spot strange things in Nevada skies. Over the years, there have been tons of UFO sightings, especially in the southern portion of the state.

MUFON (The Mutual UFO Network), received a report from a man who spotted several triangle shaped UFOs over Lake Mead during a holiday weekend in 1982.

The witness was with a group of people on a camping trip at the Lake Mead recreational area. It was May 28, Memorial Day weekend. The group arrived at the Lake Mead marina around 8:30 in the evening. They had a lot of camping gear and decided to make a couple of runs with a boat to get all their equipment to their campsite. The reporting witness, Rich, was accompanied by two other men, Reggie, and John, as they started hauling the gear across the lake. The first run would be to transport the gear, and the second run would be used to transport their fellow campers. The first run proved eventful. Rich reports:

"During the crossing, the boat hit something in the water, and it sheared the prop pin. As this has happened before, I had a spare pin, so I went over the side into the water to install the new pin. I looked up to have Reggie hand me the new pin. I saw this enormous, big black triangle with lights at each corner that seemed to be hovering over us and completely silent. I asked the others if they were seeing what I was seeing. (They) could not believe their eyes. Then we saw the two other craft that were farther away and a lot higher. We watched these craft for at least 5 minutes until they ascended upward without making any noise."

Another man wrote to me about a sighting he had along the Boulder Highway in early 1995. The witness was staying in Boulder City on business for a few days and had spent the evening in Las Vegas. He writes:

"It was about two in the morning by the time I left the strip and headed back toward Boulder City. I was wide awake, the noise and lights on the strip were always a bit much for me if I was there too long. It was the middle of the week, Tuesday or Wednesday I think, and there wasn't much traffic. I can't remember the exact date, but I think it was mid-February and I know it was 1995.

"I had the radio on, and it just stopped working. It was like the signal dropped but there was no static. The radio's lights were still on, but no sound. I was driving and messing with the buttons, trying to get the radio back on when I saw something in the air a bit in front of me. I slowed way down, thinking at first that it was an airplane, and kind of shocked that one would be so low. But it wasn't like any plane I've ever seen before. I pulled off on the side of the road and looked at it through my windshield. There were six lights on it, bright ones like lights at a ballfield."

The witness emphasized that the sighting had an unsettling quality, in part due to the complete silence that fell around him as he watched the lights.

"I remember hearing about the Phoenix lights a few years later. I don't know if that was the same thing I saw or not, and I don't know if it was an alien spaceship or what it was. Maybe it was an experimental plane that the government was testing. All I know is, it was really, really weird and I've never shaken the feeling that I saw something I wasn't supposed to see."

An August 25, 2019, report on the UFO Hunters website comes from a woman who witnessed some strange lights in the sky over Boulder City. She reports that she and her husband were staying at a hotel near the Hoover Dam when the sighting took place. The witness was sitting on a chair in front of their room while her husband had gone to retrieve something from their vehicle. Looking in the sky toward the northwest, she observed three bright lights in a row, sitting at about a 45-degree angle. She stated:

"I am used to seeing planes fly through these skies all night long, but these 3 lights were especially bright and the light in the middle appeared to flash or burn like when looking at a star."

While she was watching the strange lights, the woman also observed planes in the sky and noted the difference in their appearance to the lights she was looking at, notably, the difference in size and movement of the objects. She reported:

"The lights continued to hover over the building as if it were flying straight toward me, but then, without changing size or shape, the lights began to drift to my left. They drifted left, they dipped down a hair, came back up, drifted further left, began to head downward, then to the right. As they drifted back to the right the lights became smaller as it disappeared in the distance behind a palm tree."

The woman rushed to get behind the building and the palm tree so that she could continue to watch the lights, but when she reached a clear area, the lights had vanished.

The woman's husband returned, and she told him about the lights. They both watched the sky for a time, hoping to see the objects again, but they never reappeared.

She remains puzzled by the sighting and comments:

"I couldn't explain why the lights were so much larger than anything else in the sky, and they faced me the entire time until they disappeared."

In the fall of 2021, I spoke to a gentleman who swore that he had witnessed a large, triangular craft in the sky near Hoover Dam. The incident occurred at around two a.m. on a fall night in 2018. The witness had pulled off on the side of the road for a moment and was taking in the clear night sky when he saw the object. He said it hovered over the desert for about a minute, then shot off at an incredible speed, all in complete silence.

The man saw the shape clearly and said that it was lit along the underside edges of the triangle. He's positive it was not a known aircraft.

He was in a prime location. The outskirts of Boulder City are a great place to star gaze and if you're interested in the topic of potential alien visitation, the region is also a great place to watch the skies for UFOs.

I've personally seen some anomalous lights flying around in the sky outside of town and near the Hoover Dam. They weren't conventional aircraft, meteors, or satellites. Were they UFOs? All I know is that they were unexplainable. And I've talked to a lot of other people over the years who have also witnessed unusual, anomalous lights in the sky in the same general area.

My good friend and fellow investigator of the unknown, Joshua Warren, has observed some odd things in the skies of southern Nevada, too. Warren filmed an episode of a reality television show during which he and the film crew watched the sky with professional camera equipment. Warren and the others witnessed lights shooting through the sky that no one present could explain.

Another colleague, Steve Barone, lives on a cliff overlooking the Las Vegas Valley, and he has captured hours and hours of footage of what he believes are UFOs in the night sky. Barone is ex-military and is careful in his observations. He has a popular YouTube channel that highlights much of his footage, and if you're interested in the topic of UFOs, it's an interesting watch.

Of course, you can't visit Area 51, but Boulder City has its own headquarters for UFOs and local lore. The Aliens "R" Us Flying Saucer is a great stop for interesting souvenirs. Otherwise, be sure to look up while you're around Boulder City; the desert skies just might yield a surprise or two.

Area 51, UFOs, and the Alien Presence

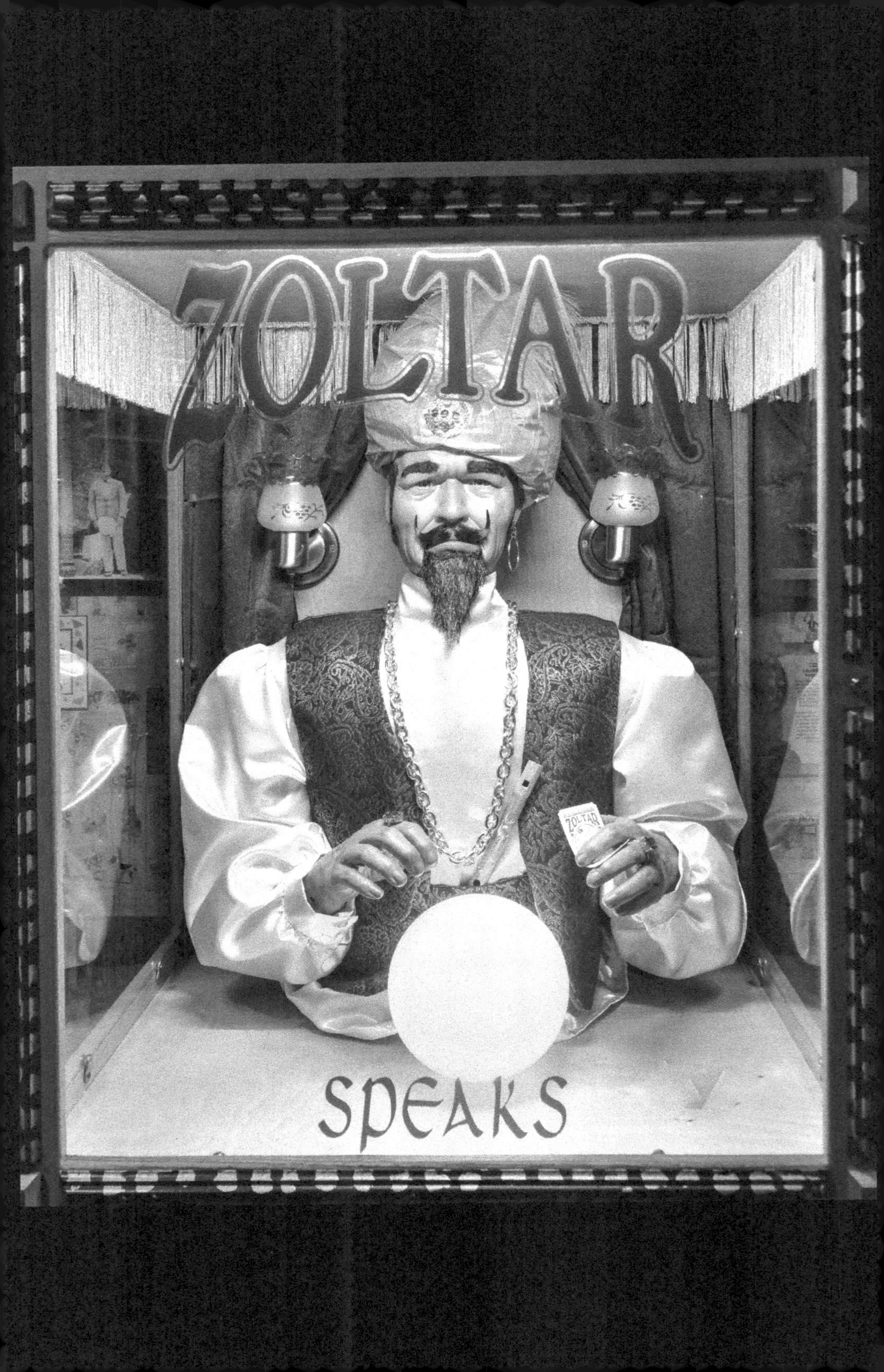
ZOLTAR
SPEAKS

I See You Over There

It may come as a surprise to learn that Boulder City has a hometown fortune teller, one that's world famous. Okay, so he's not exactly a person, but he's still pretty famous. It's none other than Zoltar, the fortune telling machine.

If you've ever walked by a Zoltar machine, you may have heard some of his attention-getting phrases such as "I see you over there!" Placing money in the machine brings it to further life and he spews out some words of wisdom and a fortune card.

Fortune telling machines have been around for a long time. The first one of note was made by the Mills Novelty Company around 1904. It was a simple affair called the "Verbal Fortune Teller." For the mere sum of a penny (it was 1904) the machine would play a recorded voice that told your fortune. Other fortune telling machines followed, including Madame Zita and Princess Doraldina, and the machines became big hits at amusement parks, on boardwalks, in arcades, and generally, in any area where tourists and vacationers were likely to spend time.

The machines never really fell out of favor, though they continued to be found mostly only at amusement areas.

In 1965 Zoltan showed up. That's right, Zoltan—not Zoltar. Zoltan was a sultan style fortune telling machine and is believed to be a direct influence for the later Zoltar.

When Zoltar came along, he was another in a wide range of animated fortune tellers with nothing particularly different. His break came in 1988 with the debut of the Tom Hanks movie *Big*. In the film, Hanks plays a twelve-year-old boy named Josh who pops a coin into a Zoltar machine and makes a wish. In

Josh's case, he wishes to be big, and the next morning, he has grown to adulthood. At least, in body. He lives out the next several weeks in an adult body trying to get back to the Zoltar machine to correct things.

The film was a hit and a turning point for Hanks whose career began to soar. Likewise, the popularity of fortune telling machines, and Zoltar in particular, began to climb. Once regulated mainly to entertainment areas, the machines started turning up at all sorts of locations, from shopping malls to convenience stores.

All those fortune tellers come from somewhere, and in this case, it's Boulder City, where Characters Unlimited produces Zoltar machines.

Olaf Stanton, owner of the company, says that every Zoltar is a custom job and great care is taken in the process. The cabinets are solid wood, crafted for durability, and come in a variety of styles. Zoltar's head is made of latex, the eyes are set in, hair and turban carefully placed, and Zoltar receives a set of teeth. But not just cheap, plastic teeth, Zoltar's chompers are cast from real human teeth—they're a cast of company owner Olaf Stanton's teeth.

Zoltar is now a nationwide hit, doling out wisdom all over the country. Since *Big*, the machine has appeared in other movies and television shows, making him a celebrity of sorts, but his home is right in Boulder City, so just remember, while you're exploring the town, Zoltar is watching!

I See You Over There

Photo Credits

Boulder Dam Hotel photo by Sarah Nichols, B&W conversion via wikicommons. File:Boulder Dam Hotel.jpg - Wikimedia Commons Creative Commons — Attribution-ShareAlike 2.0 Generic — CC BY-SA 2.0

All other photographs copyright the author or are held in the public domain.

About the Author

David Weatherly

David Weatherly is a renaissance man of the strange and supernatural. He has traveled the world in pursuit of ghosts, cryptids, UFOs, magic, and more. From the specters of dusty castles, to remote, haunted islands, from ancient sites, to modern mysteries, he has journeyed to the most unusual places on the globe seeking the unknown.

David became fascinated with the paranormal at a young age. Ghost stories and accounts of weird creatures and UFOs led him to discover many of his early influences. Writers such as John Keel, Jacques Vallee, Hans Holzer, and others set him on course to spend his life exploring and investigating the unexplained.

Throughout his life, he's also delved into shamanic and magical traditions from around the world, spending time with elders from numerous cultures in Europe, the Americas, Africa, and Asia. He has studied with Taoist masters in China, Tibetan Lamas, and other mystics from the far east. He's picked up knowledge from African and Native American tribal elders and sat around fires with shamans from countless other traditions.

Along his path, David has also gathered a lot of arcane knowledge, studying a range of ancient arts from palmistry, the runes, and other obscure forms of divination, to alchemy and magick. He has studied and taught Qigong and Ninjutsu, as well as various energy related arts. David has also studied stage and performance magic.

His shamanic and magical background has given him a unique perspective in his explorations into the unknown, and he continues to write, travel, and explore, leaving no stone unturned in his quest for the strange and unusual.

David has investigated, and written about, a diverse range of topics, including, Hauntings & Ghosts, Cryptozoology, Ufology, Ancient Mysteries, Shamanism, Magic, and Psychic Phenomena.

David is the founder of the independent media and publishing company, Eerie Lights Publishing.

He has been a featured speaker at conferences around the world and has lectured for countless paranormal and spiritual groups.

He is a frequent guest on *Coast to Coast AM* with George Noory, *Spaced Out Radio* and other radio programs. David has also appeared on numerous television shows including the Travel Channel's *Mysteries of the Outdoors*, History Channel's *Ancient Aliens, Beyond Belief* and other programs. He was also featured in the highly successful series *On the Trail of UFOs*.

David's books include *Strange Intruders, Eerie Companions,* the *Monsters of America* series, and the *Haunted* series.

Find David online at:

https://eerielights.com

Just 30 Minutes from Vegas!
An Easy, 60-minute Stroll in Historic Downtown

LEARN ABOUT:

- How many men died building the Hoover Dam & why they still haunt us

- The GHOST DOG that still wanders the streets at night

- The woman who became our first MURDERER

- Area 51 & NEW UFO Sightings!

- Where gangsters REALLY buried bodies

- Boris Karloff, Bettie Davis & strange celebs in town

- PLUS how to turn your body into a human "Ghost Meter"

- AND an ESP gambling tip!

We sell out quickly, so please book now!
Go to:
https://www.HauntedBoulderCity.com